Confetti

POEMS FOR CHILDREN

Confetti

POEMS FOR CHILDREN

poems by **PAT MORA**

illustrated by **ENRIQUE O. SANCHEZ**

SCHOLASTIC INC.

New York Toronto London Auckland Sydney

Text copyright © 1996 by Pat Mora.
Illustrations copyright © 1996 by Enrique O. Sanchez.
All rights reserved. Published by Scholastic Inc., 555 Broadway,
New York, NY 10012, by arrangement with Lee & Low Books, Inc.
Book design by Christy Hale.
Book production by Our House.
Printed in the U.S.A.
ISBN 0-590-14843-5

4 5 6 7 8 9 10   09   04 03 02 01 00 99

The illustrations are rendered in acrylic on paper.
The text is set in Frutiger.

For my daughter Libby, a sun song—P.M.

To Roberto—E.O.S.

Sun Song

Birds in the branches hear the sun's first song.
Ranitas in the rocks hear the sun's first song.
Bees in the bushes hear the sun's first song.
Wind in the willows hears the sun's first song.

Birds in the branches chirp their morning song.
Ranitas in the rocks croak their morning song.
Bees in the bushes buzz their morning song.
Wind in the willows whirrs its morning song.

Sun song. Sun song. Sun song.

Colors Crackle, Colors Roar

Red shouts a loud, balloon-round sound.

Black crackles like noisy grackles.

Café clickety-clicks its wooden sticks.

Yellow sparks and sizzles, tzz-tzz.

White sings, *Ay*, her high, light note.

Verde rustles leaf-secrets, swhish, swhish.

Gris whis-whis-whispers its kitten whiskers.

Silver ting-ting-a-ling jingles.

Azul coo-coo-coos like *pajaritos* do.

Purple thunders and rum-rum-rumbles.

Oro blares, a brassy, brass tuba.

Orange growls its striped, rolled roar.

Colors Crackle. Colors Roar.

Purple Snake

"It's in there, sleeping,"
Don Luis says and winks.
He knows I want to feel
the animal asleep in a piece of wood,
like he does
turning it this way and that,
                              listening.

Slowly he strokes the wood,
rough and wrinkled. Like his hands.
He begins to carve his way.
"*Mira*. Its head, its scales, its tail."
Don Luis rubs and strokes
the animal before he paints
its eyes open.
When the paint dries,
I place the purple snake
by the green bull and red frog
that Don Luis found asleep
in a piece of wood.

Can I, Can I Catch the Wind

Can I, can I catch the wind, in the morning, catch the wind?

Can I, can I catch the wind, in my two hands, catch the wind?

Can I, can I catch the wind, in my basket, catch the wind?

Can I, can I catch the wind, in my clay pot, catch the wind?

Can I, can I catch the wind, in my tin box, catch the wind?

Can I, can I catch the wind, in my straw hat, catch the wind?

Can I, can I catch the wind, in my bird cage, catch the wind?

Wind, Wind, run and spin, dance and spin, run and spin.

Cloud Dragons

What do you see
in the clouds so high?
What do you see in the sky?

Oh, I see dragons
that curl their tails
as they go slithering by.

What do you see
in the clouds so high?
What do you see? Tell me, do.

Oh, I see *caballitos*
that race the wind
high in the shimmering blue.

Castanet Clicks

Uno, dos
one, two
baskets blue.

Tres, cuatro
three, four
one bell more.

Cinco, seis
five, six
castanet clicks.

Siete, ocho
seven, eight
copper plates.

Nueve, diez
nine, ten
count again.

Mexican Magician

All day the *panadero*,
in white apron and ball cap,
stirs flour, eggs and sugar
then *salsas* with his broom.

His hands brim with sweet secrets,
he folds into thick fillings.
He pushes his huge rolling pin
and sings to make dough rise.

He cuts large *marranitos*
that fatten in his oven,
chops nuts, raisins and apples,
then *cha-chas* round the room.

With cinnamon and anise,
he flavors spongy dough puffs,
stirs pineapple and pumpkin
he pours in tarts and pies.

He heaps clean shelves and counters
with *pan* and *empanadas*,
pastry so light and flaky,
it sails into warm air.

His hips sway while he sprinkles
cookies with sweet confetti,
dance-dancing *panadero*,
magician with a flair.

Leaf Soup

Leaves sail through the air
like lazy *mariposas*
gliding on warm gusts
and breezes onto my hair.
Leaves spin quiet into puddles,
float on their backs then drift
                        down
                            down.

Near the prickly pear,
leaves soften into mush-clumps,
season the soup for brown squirrels
and plump birds quick hopping
to sip green
pools of tasty leaf soup.

I Hear, I Hear

I hear the rhythm of the Tarahumaras

pom, pom,

I hear them hoeing in the cornfields

pom, pom,

I hear them patting tortillas

pom, pom,

I hear them herding their goats

pom, pom,

I hear their bare feet on the land

pom, pom,

I hear them running, running

pom, pom,

I hear their steady drumbeats

pom, pom,

pom, pom,

pom, pom.

Dancing Paper

Let's fill the room with laughing
before our friends arrive.
We'll bring the colored paper.
The room will come alive.

Let's start with the *piñata*.
The air will sway and swing.
We'll string *papel picado*
to start its fluttering.

I'll fling the *serpentinas*,
toss coils in the air.
We'll add *marimba* music,
start dancing everywhere.

Remember *cascarones*,
to hide will be in vain.
Egg-bursts of bright confetti
will shower us like rain.

Abuelita's Lap

I know a place where I can sit
and tell about my day,
tell every color that I saw
from green to cactus gray.

I know a place where I can sit
and hear a favorite beat,
her heart and *cuentos* from the past,
the rhythms honey-sweet.

I know a place where I can sit
and listen to a star,
listen to its silent song
gliding from afar.

I know a place where I can sit
and hear the wind go by,
hearing it spinning round my house,
my whirling lullaby.

Words Free As Confetti

Come, words, come in your every color.
I'll toss you in storm or breeze.
I'll say, say, say you,
taste you sweet as plump plums,
bitter as old lemons.
I'll sniff you, words, warm
as almonds or tart as apple-red,
feel you green

and soft as new grass,
lightwhite as dandelion plumes,
or thorngray as cactus,
heavy as black cement,
cold as blue icicles,
warm as *abuelita's* yellowlap.
I'll hear you, words, loud as searoar's
purple crash, hushed

as *gatitos* curled in sleep,
as the last goldlullaby.
I'll see you long and dark as tunnels,
bright as rainbows,
playful as chestnutwind.
I'll watch you, words, rise and dance and spin.
I'll say, say, say you
in English,
in Spanish,

I'll find you.
Hold you.
Toss you.
I'm free too.
I say *yo soy libre*,
I am free
free, free,
free as confetti.

River Voice

In the desert, the river's voice
is cool, in canyons,
the song of rock and hawk.

In the desert, the *río's* voice
is cool, in valleys,
the song of field and owl.

In the desert, the river's voice
is cool, at dusk,
the song of star-gleam and moon.

In the desert, the *río's* voice
is cool, at dawn,
the song of wind and fresh light.

Glossary

abuelita (ah-bweh-LEE-tah): grandmother

azul (ah-ZUHL): blue

caballitos (kah-bah-YEE-toce): little horses

café (kah-FEH): brown

cascarones (kahs-kah-RONE-ehs): painted eggshells filled with confetti

cha-cha (CHAH-chah): a Latin American dance

cinco (SEEN-koh): five

cuatro (KWAH-troe): four

cuentos (KWEN-toce): stories

diez (dee-EHS): ten

dos (DOSE): two

empanadas (ehm-pa-NAH-dahs): small pies; turnovers

gatitos (gah-TEE-toce): kittens

gris (GREECE): gray

libre (LEE-breh): free

marimba (mah-REEM-bah): a musical instrument similar to a xylophone

mariposas (mah-ree-POH-sahs): butterflies

marranitos (mah-rah-NEE-toce): cookies

mira (MEE-ra

nueve (noo-WE

ocho (OH-ch

oro (OH-r

pajaritos (pah-hah-

pan (PAH

panadero (pah-na

papel picado (pah-PEHL

piñata (pee-NY

ranitas (rah-NEE

río (REE-

salsa (SAHL-sah): a L

seis (SE

serpentinas (sehr-per

siete (see-E

Tarahumaras (Tah-rah-hu-MAH-rahs):

tres (TRE

uno (OO

verde (VER

yo soy (YO